PERCEPTION

VOL 1

by: Alberto Molero

Copyright © 2025

All rights reserved. No part of this publication may be reproduced, distributed, or transmitted in any form or by any means, including photocopying, recording, or other electronic or mechanical methods, without the prior express written permission of the publisher. This restriction applies to any form or medium of reproduction or distribution. Exceptions to this rule include brief quotations that may be incorporated into critical reviews, as well as certain other non-commercial uses permitted by copyright law. Any such use must comply with the terms and permissions specified by the copyright holder.

"Happy the man... who gains understanding"
Proverbs 3.13

Prologue

Thank you for taking the time to open this book. In this world where time is precisely the most valuable thing, it can sometimes be overwhelming to decide how to dedicate it, spend it, take advantage of it, waste it, invest it, and even feel the need for it to pass slowly or quickly.

I took the time to differentiate the various things you can do with time because they are essentially the same, simply described from a different perspective.

The goal of this book is to improve the quality of life for humanity through understanding it, based on my personal approach to the philosophical question: What is the purpose of humanity? What is our reason for existing? This answer or conclusion I have reached is not entirely satisfactory because, even though it is humble and attainable, it tends to reveal the childish and selfish side within us as individuals.

This conclusion, however repetitive it may seem, is clear: to be happy.

It's often misunderstood because there are many ways to be happy, and what makes some people happy doesn't make others happy. The constant search for validation or support from others makes it difficult to achieve.

And yes! Happiness is a result, and it's the direct result of exercising our freedom. Clearly, the less free we are, the less happy we can be.

Things get more complicated when we begin to understand the world and start sacrificing our freedom, and therefore our happiness, for other things. It's no coincidence that we try to perpetuate children's happiness; it's no coincidence that we protect them so much, since we know that this combination of innocence and imagination is invaluable at that stage of life.

Well, enough of this, because it will be explained later. (TIME)Let's continue with the introduction...

This book aims to help you understand that perspective is not simply a point of view (vision), which is a serious misconception regarding the context and meaning of the word. Perspective is the understanding, comprehension, and interpretation of the reality that surrounds the being experiencing it, making use of all their senses, instincts, memories, future projections, logic, and morality.

Perspective is what connects consciousness with the cosmos.

And although ignorance is a privilege in many cases, I believe that facing reality and trying to understand its mysteries is probably the source of happiness that motivates people who change the world for the better.

It's a serious mistake to be self-guided because if we've already established that time is the most valuable thing, it makes no sense not to want to learn from others and repeat the same mistakes—perhaps not even mistakes at all. There's no need to reinvent the wheel, but I feel an urgent need to express my opinion as uninfluenced as possible.

The first book will be my personal opinion based on these 28 years of life. I plan to write a second volume after I've learned more, corrected my mistakes, and at the peak of my life, in order to set an example through study, work, and discipline. Finally, a third volume will be written when I'm older and have drawn conclusions before I die. (Beginnings - Peak - End) will clearly show how perspectives change over time. All with the sole purpose of improving our lives together on this planet.

I'm writing this book with the intention of learning from it later, as a time capsule, and as an example for myself and others of how I used to think.

I apologize in advance if my way of thinking offends anyone. My goal will never be to impose my opinion on others regarding philosophy, spirituality, or even religion.

I believe there's nothing more dangerous than being wrong and not knowing it, and that's why I've adopted a stance of always learning, correcting, improving, and evolving, taking everything—both the positive to replicate and the negative to avoid.

Perspective is also relative to time, and I think we've all noticed that we no longer think the way we used to. We've grown and learned, and that doesn't make us hypocritical or show that we've lost our essence. It's simply normal to change, and logically, to change for the better or to learn more. Many call this change maturing in life. I believe that what makes you mature isn't time itself, but the number of significant experiences within that time. Similarly, there can be 80-year-olds who have experienced less than someone who is 60.

Perspective is also contingent on time and the material conditions surrounding the individual experiencing it. And yes! Perspective is an experience, just like colors, a phenomenon that, however common and everyday it may seem, is part of one of the greatest mysteries of our existence.

Prepare to realize your worth, the value of YOUR TIME, because if there's one thing I'm sure of, it's that we don't own this collection of borrowed molecules that make up your body, and we aren't the creators of our existence. But we are the only ones who can decide what we do with our time, becoming free beings. We can also decide that our purpose is happiness, no matter how difficult it may be.

Investing our time in something is undoubtedly giving it importance, and the more importance we give something, the more powerful it becomes in our lives.

In this short book, I'm going to show you just the tip of the iceberg of the most important components that make up life as we know it, and I assure you that your life and your perception of the world will evolve for the better.

So, shall we begin?

The Beginning

I have so much to learn. I saw a really good quote that I liked…

> "*I would give everything I know to learn half of what I don't know*" **Rene Descartes**

	What i don't know that i know	**What i know that i know**
	Its when we have some kind of what it seems innate ability or when we learn something so quickly that we skip certain sequences.	Basic things or even skills that we hone in our lives, from how to dress, how to speak politely, how to drive a car.
	That's why we have to try new things; we don't know how good we are at things we've never tried.	Is what gives me certainty and make me feel that i progress and I'm learning.
	What i don't know that i don't know	**What i know that i don't know**
	This is where the errors and the danger lie.	These things are usually obvious.
	Believing we know something when its a fallacy (not knowing that you are wrong).	Like knowing i don't know how to drive a truck or a helicopter, or knit, or repair a car engine, or medicate someone.
	Its like not knowing the law; ignorance of it doesn't excuse you from obeying it or being penalized.	Accepting that i don't understand is what allows me to be humble and learn from other and from myself.
	-The number one enemy of progress. that's why we must study	

I know it's bold to tackle a topic like this at my young age (28), but I think it's time to acknowledge the era I live in and what I think as a consequence. Modernity makes us feel we know more than our ancestors, almost as if we were more evolved beings when in reality we are not.

I believe that human beings are more primitive than we want to admit, but somehow we have sought different ways to satisfy those same primitive needs to the point where we are no longer able to recognize that they are essentially the same, only with a different surface. Or, to put it another way, it's almost as if our needs evolved with us but have never left us.

Everything is the same as before; we are one species, one animal, and the passage of time has led us to adopt different customs, habits, and lifestyles, but in essence, they are exactly the same.

Survival, the struggle for power, food, understanding the world around us—everything is exactly the same, only with a different superficiality. Technological advancements have given us comforts and extended average lifespan, but at the cost of our dependence on them. Today, more than ever, we are fragile in the face of nature. What will it be like to live without electricity or the internet? We are so dependent on them that it is unthinkable to take them away from us.

The fact that there are people in the world who live without these luxuries proves they aren't necessary. However, I believe the problem with technology isn't its existence, but rather its excessive use and the squandering of resources simply to maintain comfort.

I also believe that reality exists, and truth is what allows us to approach it.

By this I mean that many people think everyone has to defend their own reality, but that's not the case. They are defending their truth, because there is only one "reality."

Conflict is inevitable when people cling to their beliefs without giving themselves a chance to understand other perspectives.

We all want to be understood in our full complexity, and we make the mistake of simplifying other people's lives, thinking only from our own perspective.

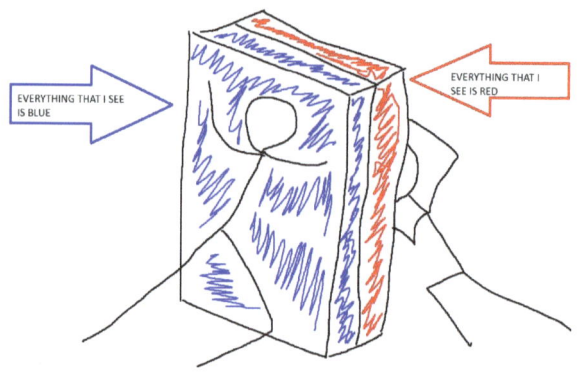

If everything we observe, remember, and feel reaffirms what we believe, it's almost inevitable that we'll be blinded by our own way of thinking. Unlearning can be one of the most painful actions; that's why we're bothered by a new boss, for example, who changes the way things are done. That's why we're bothered when we're corrected when we do something wrong. Habit and the way our neurons create memories and learning takes a significant amount of energy, and breaking those bonds to create new ones is not comfortable at all.

I believe that sometimes the best solution to a problem is the typical "agree or disagree," which doesn't fully satisfy but resolves the conflict by accepting that both sides have some valid points, especially regarding subjective matters. However, it's important to recognize the undeniable reality before us.

You can't deny the laws that govern the universe, and that's why they are laws.

You can't change the cosmos, just as you can't change your consciousness.

But you can change your perspective.

Supporting an idea, no matter how logical, obvious, or intuitive it may seem, is nothing more than a reflection of our perspective, and by adhering to it without restraint, we make a grave mistake by crushing the other person's viewpoint.

Thinking there's no other solution to a difficult problem is simply taking the easy way out.

That's why the ends cannot justify the means.

Not only is it wrong from a moral and ethical standpoint, but by ignoring other perspectives, humanity loses too much information, time, and human lives.

Like the extinction of species, cultures, and languages.

History has shown that only the victors can write it, and it makes me think how much has been lost over time.

It also makes me think about how much information has been altered. We must remember that we are heirs to all the humans who came before us. All inventions, discoveries, and advances are thanks to the fact that we live within the Continuum of intelligence of the species, and by being separated from it, we lose what we have built, forget what we have learned, and fall back into the same patterns... or at least that is the common belief.

We don't really know how much we are influenced by everything around us: alienation of thought, doctrines, subliminal messages, false information. The reality is that the world is so vast that it's ridiculous to expect to know everything for sure.

Today I write this with the intention of expressing myself fully from my core, and I know that I too have read, watched, and received all kinds of information, but before continuing to learn and be exposed to more influences, I think it's important to share my perspective.

That feeling that what I say is genuine is what I want to convey, even though we are nothing more than the accumulation of all the currents of thought that influence our lives: family, government, artists, friends—everything that is part of our lives influences the way we think, whether we like it or not. And I think that's okay, because we have to understand that in our species, and in all species, intelligence is collective. It's no coincidence that ideas are transmitted in one way or another, through books, music, movies, etc.

If you look for your favorite director, singer, or writer, they too are nothing more than an accumulation of inherited and personal ideas that make them who they are, that make them unique. And you are just as unique.

I believe that people have infinite potential; in fact, consciousness is infinite. There is no measurable amount for what you can learn. The only thing that limits this is time, and that's why it's the most important resource in existence.

Since people have infinite potential, I believe that life must be preserved at all costs. And no matter how many excuses and reasons people find to fight and kill each other—resources, territories, beliefs, or simply out of hatred—I think the worst case is when people decide to take their own lives, suicide. Yes...

I believe that everyone's life belongs to themselves and they can do with it as they please. I believe that suicide, from a perspective where there is a purpose, like that of a soldier who, when captured and knowing he will be tortured, decides to commit suicide rather than be used against his country, is one of the cases bordering on justifiable.

But suicide as an escape from life due to suffering and depression is undoubtedly the easy way out, however cruel it may sound.

And I think that the idea of not wanting to live comes from not understanding that our purpose is to be happy, or from understanding it but from the false idea that it is impossible to obtain happiness for one reason or another.

The way I see this is simple: death is GUARANTEED. In fact, life has meaning because we know we're going to die, and if death is inevitable, why rush towards it? It's going to come, whether you like it or not. There's no point in hastening the inevitable.

And I recognize that there are worse fates than death, but we must strive to make each day worthwhile for ourselves and for others, because every cell in our body seeks to stay alive, and because without others, life has no meaning.

Loving life, loving yourself, and loving others is the only way we will reach the peak of our happiness. To truly love life, it's a good idea to study it and try to understand it. To love yourself, you must understand and accept yourself, and to love others, you must do your best to understand them. All this understanding can only be nurtured by your own perspective and self-love, the perspective of others through empathy, and the perspective of God through faith.

PLEASE DON'T BE AFRAID OF THE TERM "GOD" KEEP READING!

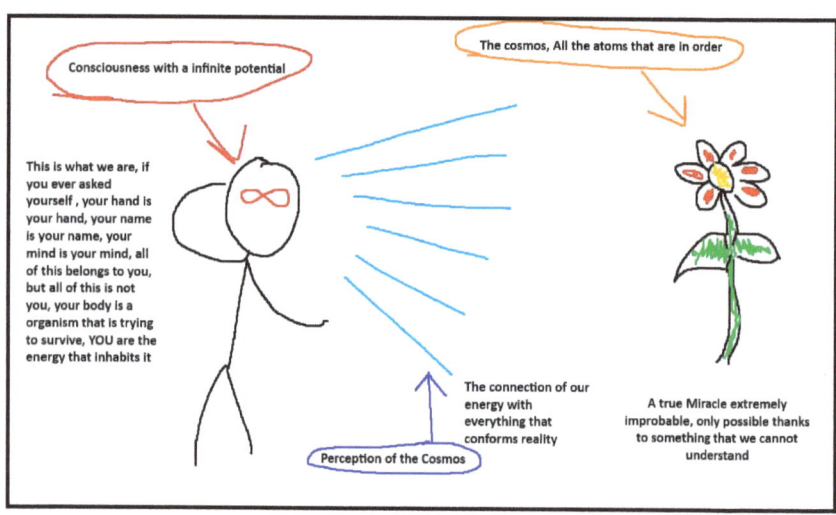

I will do my best to explain all the terms I consider necessary so that understanding what I call perception gives each of us more than one reason to love life and be grateful for it.

In the diagram above, I specify that what we are is energy. Everything else, including our own bodies, is part of the cosmos. We cannot change that energy or the matter that surrounds us. Let's remember the principle of conservation of mass and the law of conservation of energy: we cannot create or destroy, only transform. The atoms that make up your body today have existed for millions of years and will return to Earth at some point. Your energy came from somewhere, resides in your body, and will go somewhere after your death.

Since we can't change any of this, I think it's necessary to focus on what we can change, which is indeed PERCEPTION, and through this, take care of our BODY, which is our only borrowed tool, and dedicate our "TIME to what makes us HAPPY, which is each person's motivation," as Pepe Mujica said, without a logical justification... simply for the sake of being free.

The key ingredient here is the most coveted substance, yes... love.

AHA!! KEEP READING! I KNOW IT SOUNDS CORNY BUT YOU'LL SEE

Love? NO! First, we need to understand what is...

Time

Thanks to Einstein, we know that time is relative, but what does this mean?

Well, unlike the speed of light, it's not absolute and depends on the movement of the observers. It has been shown to have a correlation with gravity, but leaving the physical realm aside, have you ever noticed that time seems to pass faster or slower?

I believe that time is the RHYTHM at which our perception of the cosmos passes through our consciousness and is directly proportional to the amount of concentration and/or attention we give it. Playing a game of League of Legends or soccer, or watching a series, is not the same as looking at a microwave, or the clock on the wall to see when your shift is over, or when you're in a sauna or doing a plank during exercise. I'm not sure if we're addicted to activities that make time pass quickly, or if we're addicted to time passing quickly itself, and that's why we do these activities.

But it's true that it's pleasant when time flies by—well, sometimes. I think the idea of wanting time to adapt to our needs is a bit crazy; it's almost as if time works against us. When we want it to go fast, it goes slow, and vice versa.

So, not worrying about time is the best solution, but understanding its importance is key to being happy because one of its characteristics is that it's limited. We all have a certain amount of time available in our daily lives, and if we add to that the fact that time is divided into stages that allow us to do certain types of activities, there's no doubt that we should make the most of it.

It seems that we all come to the conclusion at some point in our lives that time is the most valuable thing, a classic feeling when we get old, also because the perception of time itself becomes longer and longer. When we are 10 years old, our whole life is 10 years, it feels like it is eternal, but when we turn 50, those same 10 years only represented 20 percent of our life, that is why we perceive that the years are passing faster simply because they represent less time in the totality of our existence.

We were born into time, and we become aware of its existence and importance as time goes on.

I believe that trying to understand time and valuing its existence makes us conscious beings.

But understanding that our time here is limited doesn't always help us grasp the importance of each experience we add to our life's catalog, to our repertoire of memories.

That's why we regret the things we didn't do when we had the chance more than the mistakes we make. Remember, the outcome can vary, and judging yourself for a bad result can help you improve, can help you change the course of your actions, but the fact that you do things is what truly matters.

Einstein said that we have to do things, even if we're bad at them, because exercising our freedom, even if it seems illogical, nourishes our energy.

UGH ENERGY, THE SECOND CORNER.

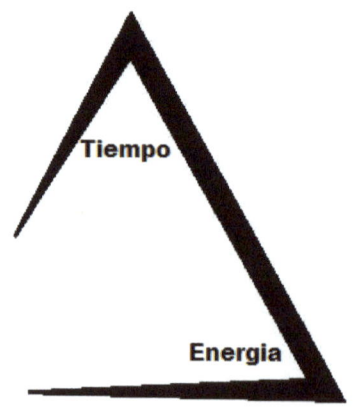

Consciusness & Energy

We define an inanimate object by observing that it lacks any of these qualities, and we identify ourselves as the supreme species because we possess these characteristics.

I believe that our lack of understanding of how the intelligence and consciousness of other species function makes us victims of our own pride.

Why are we more important than ants? Why place humanity at the top of everything when the only reason this occurs is due to our lack of knowledge? We impose our perspective on everything else when, in reality, we ignore our own circumstances. Ants have been here for 50 million years, while we have only been here for 200,000, and the most ridiculous thing is that we don't even know for sure.

All living organisms struggle to stay alive, but we have a unique ingredient, a particularity that makes us different, or at least that's what we think.

Even your own body acts in a certain way; it has defense mechanisms, dreams, anxiety, hunger—all phenomena beyond your control until you learn to manage them.

When you exercise and go to the gym to get in great shape, the reality is that it's an enormous effort and sacrifice because your body is trying to survive, and you're forcing it to fight against its own nature.

Your body stores fat and makes you gain weight in order to survive if you can't eat regularly. Often, the effect is proportional to your habits, organs, and willpower and control over your body.

Remember, your body isn't you; your body is trying to survive. You are the energy that inhabits it.

If you get used to eating smaller portions, there comes a point when your stomach reduces its size, and you feel fuller or more satisfied with less food. You can also stretch it, like professional food competitors who can eat 62 hot dogs in a competition, like Stonie and Chestnut.

Gastric bypass surgery essentially surgically reduces the size of the stomach so that the person doesn't feel the hunger reflex. And so, literally, physically, they can't eat, and mentally, they don't want to eat.

Okay, body separated from mind, now what? Well, look at this other triangle.

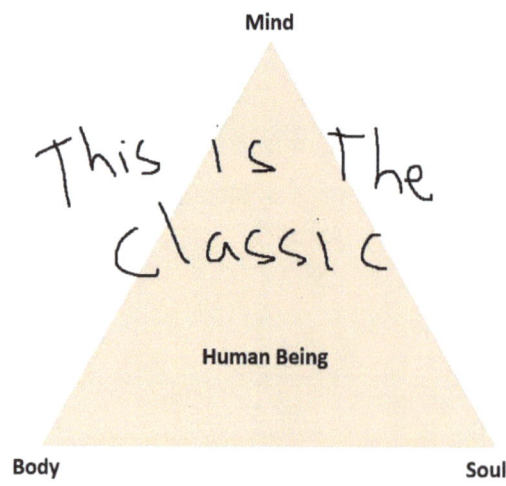

It's quite intuitive, but I think simplifying something so complex (humanity) to something so straightforward without considering that material conditions and historical context absolutely modify everything is flawed. This triangle represents the WHAT, but not the WHY. Understanding what we are doesn't give us the right to rule the universe around us. Attributing purpose to the randomness of existence has only unleashed tragedies on the planet. In the same way that we define what we are, we also assign a pseudo-value to our own species. Nationalism, racism, nepotism, and other social phenomena are the result of this fallacy.

It's effective to follow a lifestyle that embraces this triangle because you take care of your body by eating well and exercising, you read and study, you strengthen your mind, and you believe in God or have some connection to a spirituality of any kind that nourishes your soul and calms that feeling of emptiness generated by the uncertainty of our existence.

"I believe it is a great gift to believe in God and in his existence, but we cannot refuse to know science." **Canserbero**, In fact, I believe that science and the existence of a higher intelligence are closer than anything else; I even think it's more religious to be an atheist than to believe in any deity.

To conclude with the WHAT, here's my answer:

We are ENERGY ($E=mc^2$) and a collection of experiences throughout time. What I mean by this is that our energy is unique, and that's already impressive when you see the statistics of the number of people who exist who resemble you, with the same skin color, name, nationality, ambitions, and tastes. It doesn't matter how much someone resembles you or thinks like you, or even if they are identical twins; your energy is UNIQUE.

That energy depends on a substance I briefly mentioned, but which we will now explore in more detail. It is the most delicious and coveted substance, often discredited but undeniably important, if not indispensable, in life.

You can lie to me, you can lie to everyone, but you can't lie to yourself, it's impossible. As corny as it may seem, it's clear that the only thing we need to get where we want to be is...

Love

Love is undoubtedly longed for by all who have felt it; it's the fuel that motivates us. It manifests itself in different ways, but when it arrives, it can't be hidden, it can't be lied to.
Every cell in our body shows a positive change when experiencing love, and there are many ways we can feel or receive it, but here I want to start from the inside out, since self-love is the most important of all.

Because if you don't love yourself, no one else will.

Self-love is based on being yourself, doing the things you enjoy, and experiencing what you consider good. It's the most important because it defines your energy. Remember that you are nurturing your energy, and only through this can you move forward to loving your family.

When you understand that you are a special being and you take care of yourself and your freedom by cultivating your passions, you generate empathy for your family members. This is because you understand that they, like you, have these special feelings. Beyond a biological connection, your family are the energies (the people) that give purpose to your life because they share your most intimate experiences, and by developing authentically, each person gives value to their existence.

The difference between family and like-minded people is that with family you share intimacy and vulnerability. Your best friends become your family through unique and sometimes unforgettable experiences—the good times and the bad, but especially the bad, because I believe it's in those moments that a person's true character is revealed, their true colors, their true energy. **And I think the most attractive characteristic of the soul is its genuineness.**

We can appreciate and love like-minded people because they share many similarities with us: the same soccer team, the same swimming class, they like games, certain types of horror movies—any coincidence when doing an activity. Remember, that person does it genuinely, and when you connect, it's like magic, that feeling of mutual understanding, something like, "I see what you see. I have such a similar perspective that I want to stay close," making empathy easier to cultivate.

I'm not sure if love for other species is based more on innocence or the beauty of the unknown. Who doesn't love their first pet? A stray dog? Who doesn't appreciate birds in flight? There are even people who love and dedicate themselves to insects. All species on Earth have infinite value, just like us, and there are many people who don't reach this level because they assume animals don't have consciousness or feelings, when in reality, we simply haven't understood them. Just because we don't see them doesn't mean they don't exist.

> *"Our energy limits are as real as our physical limits."*
> **Carl Jung**

Animal cruelty, and the fact that we can identify it, demonstrates that empathy isn't just a human trait, but a reciprocal one between species, like when your dog or cat misses you upon your return, or when someone dies and animals become depressed.

I understand that survival and the food chain impose limits on how and when to consume animal products, but I believe that avoiding excessive violence is paramount.

The penultimate step in these layers of love is love for those who are different, which is very difficult to feel and is the reason why conflicts are sometimes resolved in the worst possible ways. It's understandable that there isn't empathy for people with different energies and even more different perspectives, such as being from a different neighborhood, a different social class, a different country, a different gender, a different culture. Because we can't understand the reasons for being of others, we often attribute them to malice, mediocrity, and madness.

"WE HAVE A VERY IMPORTANT TASK IN THE SPECIES AND THAT IS TO UNITE WITHOUT DENYING OUR DIVERSITY" **Eduardo Galeano**

And finally, we have the love of life, which I believe is the most difficult to attain because, unlike the previous layer where we have a clear path to follow, where agreements can be reached and society functions in a way that benefits everyone without the need for a common enemy.

In this last layer there isn't exactly one path, but many. This layer is about the love of life regardless of how irrational, cruel, and uncertain it may be, where we face natural disasters, acts of terrorism, phenomena of violence within society, illnesses, and supernatural events that have no explanation or valid purpose.

We ask ourselves WHY these things happen, why my son died in an accident that had nothing to do with him, why this baby got this disease, why God allows things to happen. It's so difficult to reach a point where all these things make sense that all sense of justice is lost.

I believe that 99% of the disasters that have occurred and continue to occur in humanity are the product of human actions, an evil that, due to a lack of the development of love at all levels, generates unjustified suffering: the Holocaust, the Twin Towers, Hiroshima and Nagasaki, as well as dictatorships, mafias, serial killers, among many other things.

It's important to remember that the existence of evil is what makes us free. We are all capable of wrongdoing, but some of us choose not to, whether due to ethical or moral values, fear of God, or remorse. The choice must exist; otherwise, our existence would be meaningless.

God created a world governed by unchanging physical laws and gave us free will. Those who commit evil are simply free individuals, lacking any regard for values like empathy, respect, and cooperation. Some of these actions stem from mental illness, but ultimately, it is thanks to this freedom that we are free and that life has meaning. Consider examples like Psycho-Pass or A Clockwork Orange.

The key to loving life and mastering this final layer is FAITH. Simply have FAITH that God knows why He does things, because I think it's impossible to believe in a god we can fully understand; His perspective is beyond the imagination of any human.
And it doesn't matter what name you give your God, or if you prefer to call it a higher intelligence, or whatever, as long as the layers of love don't contradict each other, I believe any culture is correct. Faith is necessary to be HAPPY.

Freedom and Happiness

They are directly proportional.

I already said that happiness is the direct result of exercising our freedom, and by this I mean that it is our choice, our contribution, our intervention in reality that makes us feel special. No matter how much you enjoy doing something, being with someone, or eating something, if you are forced to do it, if it's not your choice, it loses its magic and its energy.

There is nothing worse than a forced marriage. We don't like being forced to go to school as children, and our parents do it because our perspective is so naive and innocent that it's an action within the bounds of what is justifiable. The fact that we don't like something doesn't mean we should never try it. In the end, it's all about new experiences and understanding perspectives that are foreign to us. But when something is imposed on us, no matter how logical, productive, or beneficial it may be, it's impossible for us to be happy with it. If life gives you lemons, make lemonade, they say, but if I hate lemons, there's no way I'm going to be happy doing that. Even if you're the son of a family of doctors, engineers, or lawyers, if your energy doesn't want any of that, there's no way it will make you happy.

> "Like Vito, Michael, and Anthony Corleone. Let's learn from them.".
> **The Godfather Saga**

Throughout history, there have been many detriments to freedom, some more obvious than others, such as slavery, dictatorships, and monarchies, but none as destructive and harmful as those found in our current capitalist and democratic society, because these systems, in essence, deprive us of the opportunity to combat them at their root.

If I am a slave, and the reason for my slavery is that I am Black and have a shackle on my leg, the solution is to fight or die. But if I am unaware that I am a slave, there is no escape from the cubicle I inhabit.

"Are you truly free? Or are you a slave to consumer society? Remember that the MONEY you earn is earned with the TIME of your life that you invested to obtain it."**Pepe Mujica,** And remember, from the beginning I already said that TIME is the most important and invaluable RESOURCE in life.

How much is your time worth? Well, it depends on where you are on the planet, it depends on who you know, it depends on what you know how to do. It's very easy to feel content when you get paid more for what you do, but the people who are truly happy are those who don't sell a single second of their time for something that doesn't fulfill them —very privileged people who are happy outside of a society that only seeks MONEY.

> "Happiness has been confused with excessive money, when life slips away without turning back."
> **Canserbero**

And when you combine this mentality with the Wasteful Generation, you find a more damaged and depressed world, where there's no way out because there's no other system. Those who control the system entertain others with content and false hopes of reaching the top. Happiness isn't there; happiness is here. You just have to change your perception.

Criticizing the system will always offend those who are part of it. I believe there are exceptional people who, through effort, discipline, and perseverance, have achieved everything they've set out to do. But the pursuit of money above all else is the reason for so much depression globally and explains why, in global suicide statistics, comparing countries by their wealth, what this insatiable pursuit of money generates is nothing more than the loss of inner energy. And without that energy, we cannot live, we cannot be happy, we cannot love.

A necessary evil?

MONEY

Well, if you've made it this far, I think you're ready to read what I think about money, and I don't want to sound ridiculous by saying I don't want it, because in the end, money gives you peace of mind, and it gives you a sense of security and stability. "I also want my house with a pool, but I'd much rather not see any more children on street corners." **Canserbero**

And you?

Money is necessary for the functioning of modern society, and that's the only thing I appreciate about it. But when I see so much time and energy being exchanged for something as useless as money, it really pisses me off. Because yes, it gives you comforts you sometimes don't even need, it gives you fun and peace of mind, but you can't really buy anything of value with it. You can buy things that cost a lot but are WORTH NOTHING.

You can buy a plane, a bigger house, a faster car, and all that's fine, but... you can't buy time, because it doesn't stop and nobody owns it.

You can't buy love

> *""not even the cheapest whores sell their 'I love yous'"*
> **Canserbero**

You can't buy friends, you can't buy the feeling of satisfaction that comes from earning things, because happiness isn't about having them, it's about striving for them and deserving them.

Everything that truly matters can't be bought with money. I know we have to pay the bills, I know we have to survive in society, but be very careful about exchanging what's most important for something so frivolous and meaningless.

I believe everyone on Earth wants the same thing, but we're separated by language.

> *Like at the Tower of Babel*
> **Génesis 11:1-9**

언어

If you don't know the language in which the philosophy is being described, there's no way you can understand its PERSPECTIVES.
Like colors, perspective is an individual experience, but how do we communicate? If Perspective is the information I perceive, that the cosmos sends me and that I interpret in some way, how do I interact back?

Well, clearly through language! Verbal and non-verbal. Learning which words signify which feelings is difficult; transmitting that across generations and trying to understand each other depending on the different civilizations that make up the planet is a very hard task.

I wish a group of polyglots who not only know the language but also the culture of each country could agree to create a language, a single language that everyone speaks so that we can all understand each other better.

Today I feel like writing the best book in the world, one that will be translated and understood worldwide.

I love the Spanish language because it's richer for describing and specifying things, and I love English because it's fast and adaptable. I like to take the best of both languages, even if it means making a grammatical error.

PERCEPTION

But even so, in any language in the world, it's clear that we all have similar behavioral patterns, and challenging this need for love and the revitalization of our energy can affect us greatly, to the point that our minds are filled with negative ideas that distance us from what's good for us. That's why we must study, that's why we must read, that's why we must experiment, and not just blindly follow popular trends and religious and nationalist indoctrination.

The mind is very fragile, and trying to understand the world around us, when it contradicts different ways of thinking and different ways of shaping reality, creates a divergence in our own perception of reality, so much so that we can even reach the point of losing ourselves.

"Sometimes I feel ignored or misunderstood by these masses who embrace what is meaningless"
Canserbero

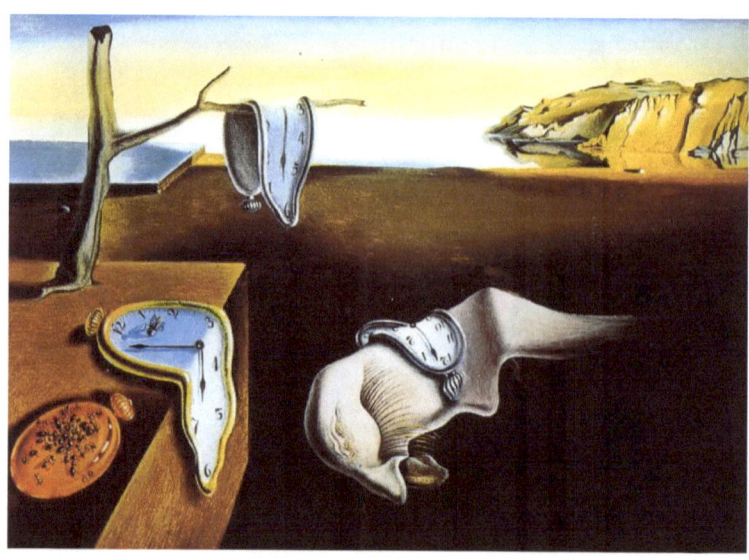

¿Am I crazy? Or is everyone crazy?

I think anyone who has ever doubted themselves has asked this question, but I always like to remember a phrase that goes like this...

"The only difference between Dalí and a madman is that Dalí is not mad."
Salvador Dali

When we perceive the world in a way that no one else does, we are inevitably misunderstood. However, we may generate admiration from those who cannot see it as we do, as well as rejection from those who refuse to accept that it is simply a different perspective, not a fallacy that threatens their sanity.

When a person has a worldview, an idea, a creative impulse, they inevitably seek to express and embody it in a work of art, a film, a song, a book, captivating those who believe they understand it (scientists are artists too) and repelling those who are not drawn to it. In the end, it is simply a different perspective, not an approach to the truth that endangers reality and order.

I believe that people experience changes in their worldview over time, and this is especially true when they are introduced to the world of drugs, or any substance that alters their perception of the world.

Drugs

Well, I think the first thing to understand is that any substance that alters how you feel is a drug, from sugar to hard drugs that literally put you in a state where you disconnect from reality as we know it.

The worst drugs are the ones you buy at the supermarket; it's just that their normalization has made us unaware of the impact they have on our lives.

If we're going to judge them by their potential harm, then we have to look at the statistics.

A comparison of the real damage that drugs do to their users and to other people.

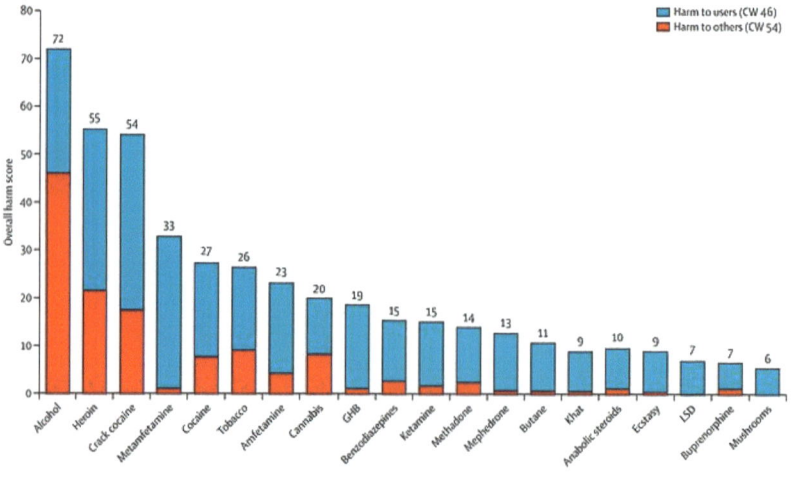

David Nutt (The Lancet)

I think our minds are more fragile than we realize. Our brains are constantly trying to process all the information that comes in nonstop, all day, every day. Exposing them to excessive substance abuse inevitably causes damage, especially to young people. Studies say the brain develops until age 26, which I think is a reasonable age to enter this world. I don't want anyone to start doing drugs after seeing this, but ask yourself, how addicted are you to junk food and sugar? The sugar in orange juice is just as bad as the sugar in ice cream, as is caffeine every morning and alcohol on weekends.

With opioids and antidepressants, it seems people don't understand that just because something is accepted doesn't mean it's good or better; it simply means it's not immediately negative, but it's certainly negative in the long run.

And now, in the realm of psychoactive drugs, I think the term "high" is pretty self-explanatory. It involves the feeling of being elevated or a perspective enhancer, where you see the world through a different lens, where substances in our brain activate connections that wouldn't otherwise be active, or not to the same degree.

This shift in perspective can teach you a lot. Seeing something differently changes your entire understanding of it, but we must be clear that it's an individual experience, and in the realm of the mind, which is so unexplored and uncertain, we can't validate the knowledge that drugs give us with certainty.

Using drugs is somewhat selfish because you go to a different place alone. That's why people use drugs with friends or in groups, so everyone can experience the trip together.

Drugs should be used as rewards, not crutches.

That's why we drink to celebrate a victory, passing an exam, or any achievement—we celebrate with substances and fun to be "a little bit out of our minds."

All drugs have a correct way of interacting with them. The best way is not to interact with them at all, but satisfying curiosity is the priority, since in the end we are free, so it should be done with the utmost care, respect, and possible help from friends, doctors, or specialized personnel.

So many different perspectives generate the most absurd things: divisions within the species... and it's logical. A lot of beings see the world, and each one interprets it differently. If you add drugs to this mess, well, there comes a point where the truth is completely distorted.

Racism isn't about color; it's about culture. Only by understanding other cultures' perspectives can we truly grasp the sick nature of racism. It's literally hating something you don't know simply because it's different.

It's like saying, "I like chocolate ice cream and I hate strawberry because it's pink." You don't like it because it's pink, you hate it because it's strawberry, and you take your attraction to a very personal and senseless level.

The world has so many things; obviously, there are things you won't like, people with different energies, unpleasant situations that we have to face every day in the everyday life of society.

WE MUST UNITE, WITHOUT DENYING OUR DIVERSITY. **Eduardo Galeano**

Imposing our truth on others, like people who say they identify differently simply because they feel that way, is a grave mistake and we must not allow it to continue. Any argument that contradicts the reality most of us perceive should not be taken seriously. We barely understand the cosmos as it is; imagine if we had to adapt it to everyone... if you are a man, you are a man; if you are a woman, you are a woman. Every cell in your body already has that genetic code, and there is no way to change it.

You can dress as you like, call yourself whatever you like, but don't expect others to treat you the way you perceive yourself, because it is a selfish endeavor and only undermines the functioning and progress of society.

"Attraction is not an election" **Mario Luna**.
That's why there are straight people and gay people; to each their own.

"But your freedom ends where the freedom of the other begins" **Dross.**

Don't try to defy the physical and natural laws that govern us.

PERCEPTION

Natural Laws

The constant, consistent, and governing variables are the precepts that individuals must follow to survive in the state of nature. These laws include physical laws and empirical knowledge, which is based on experience. Ultimately, empirical knowledge is our perception of the world, telling us what exists and what its characteristics are.

One of my favorites is Murphy's Law, which, despite its humorous approach, is undeniably true. Other examples include Karma and the Law of Attraction.

Just like these, in the "concrete jungle" **Hector Lavoe** There are many official laws, subliminal laws, and codes of honor that we must follow in order to survive and to progress.

Where those who don't adapt don't survive, and those who threaten peace are stripped of their most important value:

Freedom.

In a more global sense,

Humanity depends on so many variables for its existence that it is undoubtedly a miracle, and each individual life contributes to that miracle simply by winning the sperm race.

And if we touch upon the law of causality, I think we encounter the central theme of all philosophical topics: our origin.

When we trace our origins back linearly, there is no answer that satisfies everyone, and any theory that might be attributed to this phenomenon of life on our planet is, I believe, far from being understood. We need to prioritize other things to make the world a better place. The level of intellect we must reach as a species to understand our origins is only comparable to that of a god.

God

In this causal world, there exists something uncreated that unites everything. And since the world is filled with intelligent, conscious beings and immense natural and cosmic beauty, we can only attribute positive value to that which unites it or to that which created it—a value to its intelligence that we cannot comprehend.

I choose to give it the name inherited from my entire family and culture, but I understand that no matter what name we give it, there is a god that we cannot confine within our primitive understanding of the universe. Names, images, numbers—none of that. But since it is what we, as quasi-divine human beings, understand, it is the closest we have to describing it.

I believe that the greatest sense that compels me to believe in the existence of a higher intelligence is the amount of chaos that inhabits our universe. Order is so minimal that it is literally a miracle.

It's more likely you'll win the lottery 200 times in a row, once in each different country, than that our lives will be possible.

And after many years of being agnostic, I think I've absorbed so much scientific evidence that the existence of God is undeniable to me. The more you study science, the more you delve into the facts that keep us alive, the more undeniable His existence becomes.

It's more religious to be an atheist than a believer.

But if God is perfect and He created a world with laws that don't contradict each other, I think I could venture to say I understand something about Him, and that is that He is based on the perfect combination of variables so that things in disorder become ordered.

The closest thing to perfection is BALANCE, and we can clearly see this balance of proportions in everyday life, in formulas that are valid through equality (=), in chemical equivalencies, among other things...

BALANCE

This is key. I believe that 99% of everything that works in our lives depends on a certain balance—relationships, nutritional values, lifestyles—and when that balance is disrupted, there are consequences that are usually negative.

The opposite of balance is excess. To rephrase this, everything in excess is bad. I believe this is absolutely true, and when I apply it to any example, the result is almost always negative. No matter how good something is in itself, in excess it ends up causing bad results.

Apply this to your life and you'll undoubtedly see improvements: balance in your diet, balance in your relationships, balance at work, balance in how you manage your time.

Remember, your time is the most important thing, and through balance and its proper allocation, you'll reach the peak of your life while you're on this earth.

And I know it's difficult, but you must understand that you're accustomed to what the world offers. We're addicted to sugar from a young age, addicted to pornography from adolescence, and addicted to money when, as adults, we realize it's what's needed to solve problems. But all of this is not necessary, and if quitting isn't an option, we must do our best to find balance.

It's difficult to maintain balance, which is why only the most exceptional members of our species achieve it, since we face a world of chaos and inexplicable, unpredictable situations every day.

But I think these situations are what keep us alive, what keep us wanting more, what gives us that feeling of curiosity to discover a new day, a new person, a new game. It's as if we're addicted to this feeling, and I'm so grateful that it's this way, as if life were a puzzle we're trying to solve, only you have to decide which perspective you choose for your life.

My grandmother told me, "Son, you're grabbing the ember by the coals," and what she means is simple: I'm choosing to see things from a negative point of view, and I suffer when I get stuck in that thinking.

And speaking of her, I think it's time to tell one of the best stories I like to share, one that changed my life for the better and that I'm grateful for today.

I was in Maracaibo, without electricity, in sweltering heat, not knowing where my mother was, far from my father, far from my siblings, alone with my grandmother, hungry because without water we couldn't cook, frustrated because the country's situation was getting worse and worse.

The career I chose didn't satisfy me, or my family, and all I was looking for was money. My professors were malnourished, and if they were my role models, what hope was there for me?

I went to her room and told her, "Grandma, I feel awful. Everything is a mess. How can people not realize that it's all a charade and that we're so helpless? I hate what we're going through because it makes no sense."

She told me, "Son, there's the tree... go hang yourself." The shock of her certainty illuminating my mind made me smile and say, "Oh, it's not that big of a deal..." And the truth is, it's never that big of a deal!

What's one more stripe on a tiger?

I had her, I had a roof over my head, I had my aunts and uncles, and my family who, even though I didn't see them often, were working hard so we could all be better off. I got so caught up in thinking my life was shit when, in reality, I was privileged.

LAMP 12 AUG 1997

Since we're talking about me, I want to write a mini-biography or brief history. I was born in Maracaibo. I don't know exactly when I became aware of my surroundings, but I remember that we moved to Maracay when I was six. I remember living in Montaña Fresca, and then traveling to Peru for two years. I lived in Lima, and it's the first time I remember how different life is in another country—the food, the way they spoke, everything I was used to was different. It was an incredible stay. Then, at nine, I returned to Venezuela, to a more modest school, and then I transferred to Calicantina, where I spent most of my years. I've always said that the most important thing I took away from school, and the reason it was all worthwhile, are my friends, my brothers and sisters for life, whom I miss and who are my motivation to keep going. After graduating, I moved back to Maracaibo out of fear. I had at least three experiences where we were kidnapped in our own homes, victims of organized crime,In the midst of my studies, the country's crisis intensified to the point where the stress and what my university friends and I called "the country's crisis" became overwhelming.

The unhappiness was evident, and my grandmother's story opened my mind. When my brother, who bravely decided to emigrate, was having a hard time, I decided to leave the country too.

But it wasn't until I spoke with my uncle Jose, my role model, that I felt truly moved. He told me, "Do you know why I am where I am? Because I do what I want. Now you have to do what you want! Stop trying to please me, your father, or anyone else. There are problems here and there, but you have to face the problems you want to face, not the ones others want you to face." To this day, I continue to do so, and I don't intend to return empty-handed.

Throughout my life, I've always felt alienated for thinking differently. I'm always in the middle. When my parents divorced, I was caught in the middle, neither taking sides. I'm the middle child, following in my older brother's footsteps and protecting my younger sister. When it comes to politics, it's either left or right. It sucks to be neutral, but I can't help it. If I'm not completely convinced of something, I don't accept it, since all schools of thought have pros and cons, but they don't have to be the only ones.

Being neutral is a struggle because people in the world operate on the principle of "if you're not with me, you're against me," and I think that's a mistake. The world doesn't have to be black and white. I believe there's a spectrum of gray in between that should allow us to make the best decisions.

I am an existentialist, I believe in God, I hate politics, and I don't believe in democracy. I choose not to be part of those systems that lie to us and don't really care about us.

The philosopher **Søren Kierkegaard** is considered the father of existentialism. He determined that each individual is responsible for finding meaning in their own existence. He added that the greatest responsibility of human beings lies in living their own lives passionately and sincerely, despite the countless obstacles that may arise.

I'm copying and pasting this here to clarify what existentialism is. I also want to add a touch of what Ángel David Revilla always preaches: your freedom ends where the freedom of others begins. Therefore, you can do whatever you want with your life as long as you don't ruin the lives of others. We all try to climb the ladder, but we can't do it by undermining others. And we must also understand that... YES!! You are an individual being, but there are people around you who love you, and if they don't understand you, you should try to make your perspective clear.

Finally, I want to remember my dad, who told me in his office the last time I saw him in person, "I don't understand you, nor do I support you, but I respect you. Do what you have to do; you will always be my son, and I will always love you."

I believe that respect is the most important thing that should prevail among all people in order to find peace in life and death.

Life & Death

Life is all that we know, and death is simply the opposite; life is everything that enters our collection of memories—essentially, everything that can be remembered or imagined is present in life. "He who leaves does not die; only he who is forgotten dies.."**Canserbero**

If you analyze each characteristic of life and place it on the other side of the equation, like in a mathematical formula, you find the characteristics of death. For example, life is limited, death is eternal; life is effort, death is rest, among other things.

The point here is that I believe we, who are energy, inhabit this body, and when the moment arrives and our energy is ready to go to death, it will be nothing more than a transfer to another plane, another life, whose characteristics will be defined by the way you live on Earth.

Everything you do in life you will pay for in death, because in a world where justice seems absent in many areas, death brings balance. That's why we have this tendency to believe in heaven and hell.

Whatever comes next, I'm sure everyone will get what they deserve, so strive to deserve the best, to be the best version of yourself in your time, and to love, because life is limited, death is certain, and the only thing that is eternal is the MESSAGE we transmit to others.

The Message

Intelligence is collective, and by this I mean that we are all connected in a way that transcends conventional communication. Intelligence is a phenomenon determined by the outcome of our actions and is contingent upon the time and context of the situation or the person performing the actions.

We don't attribute a lack of intelligence to someone living in a less technologically advanced tribe; it's simply a lack of a long line of inheritors of the MESSAGE and the experiences of their ancestors.

If you fall into a hole, you suffer, you survive, you learn from it, and only if you are intelligent will you avoid falling again. But if you go further, you can make a sign that says, "Beware, there's a hole here," and through your effort and by perpetuating the message through your actions, your experience and intelligence will be inherited by others. Even if you die, the rest of humanity will understand that there's a hole there, and thanks to you, accidents, among other things, will be avoided.

The message can be something that endures beyond our ephemeral existence; it's our way of achieving immortality through texts, music, physical works, actions, and creations that last beyond our time. That's why it's so important to leave our mark on the world.

My father told me, "Every man should plant a tree, write a book, and have a child." I think this advice shouldn't be taken so literally. What he means is that we should strive to contribute some of our intelligence to society and the human race. Maybe you're not a writer, maybe you're not an actor, maybe you don't do anything particularly well, but you work and have money.

Well, there are also good fans who support artists, and it's only through your help as a fan, or as someone who offers support in some way, that these people are able to bring their work into the world.

The most important thing is ACTION!

GUIDE FOR ACTION

Just as we can decide to change our perspective, we can also take action. Thinking about and analyzing situations gives us the opportunity to make the best decision, but the reality is that if you wait too long, time will pass and you won't be able to do anything.

Not too early, not too late—it's difficult, and that's why so few exceptional people manage to overcome the system and achieve a lifestyle where they spend most of their time in a constant flow of productivity and well-being. Meanwhile, there are people who suffer from depression from inaction. The worst enemy of the self is "what if," and the best friend is action.

I'm sure the feeling of remorse that affects you most is that of POSSIBLE PAST THINGS, what would have happened if? Torturing yourself thinking about this is nothing more than masochism, but there comes a point when you can no longer bear it and you have to start doing something. Some people have moments of shock that awaken them, usually after a tragedy or illness, but why wait for something so drastic to happen when what you have to do is act, lock in, and do things with love, discipline, respect, patience, and gratitude? Because if anything is certain, just like death, it's that things can always get worse. There is no stronger regulator of your mood than the perspective from which you choose to view your life.

There will always be people in better or worse situations, there will always be rich and poor. You can be happy without money, but you can also be happy with money; there's no reason why not. The problem is when we confuse happiness with excessive wealth. Life will slip through your fingers as you chase one or the other. Balance, as we've already discussed, should be the way you organize your life.

Imagine you could see your entire life in a single image, or wait... you can!

MEMENTO MORI

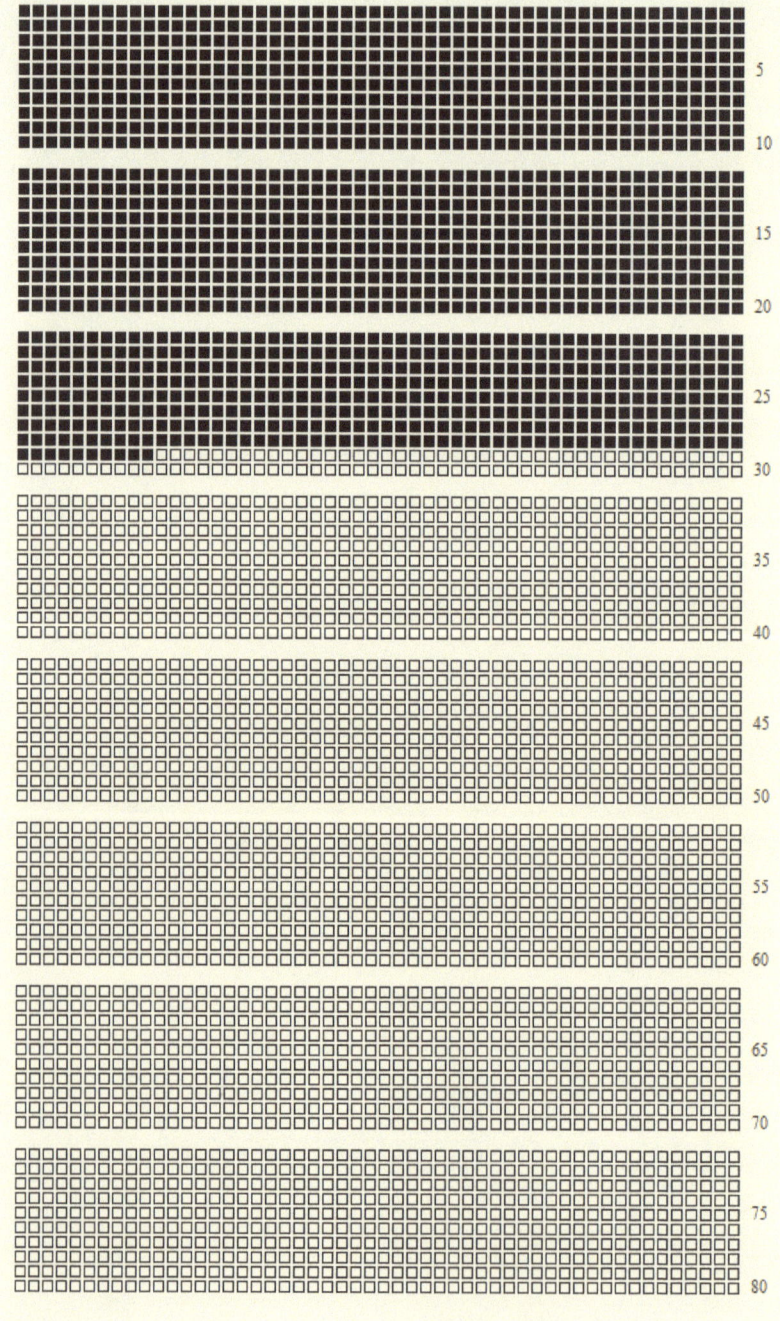

PERCEPTION

This is my "memento mori," my lifespan. I was born on August 12, 1997. Each square represents a week of my life, and look how few I have left! I plan to live at least 80, so there's no more time to waste.

I invite you to fill in each square until you reach your age.

What matters is tomorrow, so be grateful and dream!

Remember with love all that you have done, and work today to eliminate that "what if" once and for all.

Death will be another adventure, who knows?

But while you have life, it's time to make the most of it.

Only by making the most of our time can we improve the future of our country.

Future of Venezuela

I've always thought that being proud of where you're from is pointless because there's no merit in simply being born somewhere, or being a man or a woman., "White, black, yellow, or red, if skin color doesn't matter more than the color of your eyes." **Canserbero**, All these attributes, when overvalued, generate racism, nationalism, and fascism, and are nothing but nonsense.

However, where I was born is inevitably part of my history and is my only tool with which to face the world. Long ago, my uncle Arecio and I determined that your life is defined by three variables: genetics, geography, and the time in which you live. It's not the same to be born Venezuelan in 2015 as it is in 1980; it's not the same to be Jewish today as it was in 1945; it's not the same to be Muslim after 9/11; it's not the same to be born in the United States as it is in Venezuela or Guinea-Bissau; and obviously, it's not the same to be born with all your limbs, your eyes, your senses, and without any health problems that affect the normality of your life.

However, Michael Melamed has taught us that regardless of adversity, difficulties, statistics, intuition, and expert logic, things can be achieved as long as we take ACTION.

I believe that being an immigrant from a country where, from the beginning, I interacted with Peruvians, Italians, Americans, Chinese, Portuguese, Lebanese, Spaniards,

Africans, and Germans, and growing up so familiar with all these cultures...

"It has undoubtedly made us the most privileged citizens in the world, because a Venezuelan has the greatest capacity to understand humanity; we should use that right to culture that history has given us." **Jose Ignacio Cabrujas**

In this present moment, with this shitty crisis my country is experiencing, I have no doubt that a better future awaits us, since all of us who left are only learning the best and worst of all cultures around the world, as if spreading around the world were to sow and cultivate experiences.

Leaving your country, traveling, and experiencing other cultures is probably the most privileged thing you can do, because it allows you to see the world from a completely different perspective. You humbly learn how small your community and country really are. When you're aware of the world's immensity and the diversity of ways of thinking, it's inevitable to feel more humble and curious, especially since everything is done differently.

I always hated eating with a serrated knife and fork to cut a steak on a glass plate. When I started eating Korean ramen, kimchi, egg gooey, kimbap, and bibimbap, and learned to eat with chopsticks and how convenient they are, it was another shift in perspective. I'm taking the best from each culture.

God, if only I could try the best dish from every country, have a conversation with someone from every country, and listen to a song in every language.

The point is simple: the immense amount of intelligence accumulating from all the immigrants who are learning about the new systems they work for will undoubtedly enrich our country in return. All that's needed is someone to set an example and, in some way, brave people willing to rebuild what has been destroyed.

"There can be no revolution without an evolution of consciousness."**Canserbero**

And this is the best opportunity, one where we all start from scratch outside and learn from the shit and the discrimination.

"Not only is a change of government needed, but what's really lacking here is for us to start reading and using our notebooks.."**Canserbero**

I wish all schools would pay more attention to philosophy subjects, and in Venezuela, that we would listen more to what Arturo Uslar Pietri teaches us. By setting an example in our country, we can improve the region and the world. We cannot fall into the selfishness of only wanting peace for ourselves; we must help others.

We cannot allow more misery and wars (Russia-Ukraine).

Future of the world

We're all in this together on this spaceship, oscillating through the universe, and I think sooner or later we tend to unite as a species. But the most common scenario is one of tragedies and common enemies. It seems as if in the future, most scenarios are apocalyptic: too much nuclear aftermath, resource scarcity, wars, and mass genocide.

One of my favorite examples is the science fiction film Starship Troopers (it's a satire of authoritarianism, fascism, and militarism). I watched it on Venevisión when I was a kid, and I think that movie is what made me obsessed with redheads for life. I think it was the first time I saw such divine breasts. But the connection between that movie and this comment is the unity of the entire planet, practically a utopia. And when you think about equality or equity for humanity, I start thinking about a specific scene.

Aside from the perfect tits, what's truly remarkable is that all these people, men and women, are showering together, without excessive sexualization.

There are white, Black, Hispanic, and Asian people, and they're all talking about why they're there. Some want to join the army for a scholarship, others for government benefits, others for money.

The point here is, imagine the level of coexistence and respect that can be achieved when society focuses on what truly matters: the progress of humanity, the planet, and all the species that inhabit it.

And remember, no matter how individualistic your motivation is, as long as it's satisfying and respect prevails above all else, I think it's a valid reason to use your time, YOUR TIME. And now that you understand all this...

What will your action be?

Plan of Action

I want you to write down your action plan here—whatever you have in mind, short, medium, and long term. This is your book now, so write it down

_____
_____
_____
_____
_____
_____

Since simply writing things down helps us understand them differently, and the habit of writing has been lost with so much technology, I want to give everyone a chance to do it.

Everyone has their own formula for success; what matters are the results.

Come back here when you've made it.

We're almost at the end of this experience. I'm going to give you what I value today, what I learned through pain. But first, you must understand that no matter what you've written here, no matter if you find a way to improve the world without consequences, no matter how good your intentions are, you will always have new enemies.

So beware of envy.

Don't tell anyone if you have to.

Take action.

Don't just say you're going to do things, just do them!

New enemies

The world is full of all kinds of people, and just like you, some may or may not understand all these concepts that make up society, and you must understand that they don't necessarily have to agree with whatever you have in mind, no matter how logical or altruistic it may be, and that's completely normal.

YOUR GREATEST ENEMY IS YOU., YOU AGAINST YOU

Slayer

Recognizing that we are our own biggest obstacle takes time, especially when we realize that others can move forward under similar or even worse circumstances.

However, mastering and acknowledging our own situation isn't the only problem we face. You are your own worst enemy, but you're not alone. The people around you are also searching for what you're searching for: happiness, financial freedom, pleasure, reaching the top—whatever they might set their minds to.

Life is a race, as David Gomez told me. Life is a race where we all try to reach a finish line, and people start at different distances from it. Some have more advantages, some have fewer, and you're somewhere in between.

Respect is simply running in your own lane, learning to run, learning to breathe, but not sabotaging others.

Because what matters is not reaching the finish line, it's doing your best to run it, giving your best effort, deserving to win it, and enjoying running.

Respect your enemies, learn from them, and become the best version of yourself. Only then will you reach your goal. And sorry for the spoiler, but what you call your goal... hahaha... it doesn't end there... when you get there, you'll laugh. **Laugh Tale?**

I want to give an honorable mention once again to evil, or what we consider evil in the world, and it is thanks to this that we are free and that life has meaning. There are more good people in the world, but evil is very noisy and that is why it is more noticeable. We all make mistakes, but we must do our best not to repeat them. We must concentrate on causing the least amount of pain to others and concentrate on causing the greatest amount of pleasure to ourselves at the same time.

The greatest pain: it has to do with injustice, with an undeserved consequence. That's why it hurts so much when someone is wronged, or when natural disasters or childhood illnesses occur. When pain is unjustified, it's what hurts us most deeply.

We feel good when we execute pedophiles, murderers, extortionists, rapists, thieves, and any of these perpetrators because we feel they deserve it.

The greatest pleasure: many say it's sex, many say it's food, others say it's peace. I think all of these are the most noticeable in a physical sense, but when we access them through improper methods, they will never be truly satisfying. That's why there's an important distinction between having sex and making love. That's why good nutrition and balance allow us to enjoy food more, and that's why we can't achieve the "Post-War Dream."

It seems that the correlation between deserving what one has and doing the right thing truly defines what a person contributes to life.

I think the best advice I've ever heard is from Roger Waters' mother, and it's simple: when you encounter a problem, you have to do two things. First, study it, analyze it, learn about it, ask questions, investigate, do everything possible to understand it and learn from it.

And then, once you've finished this work, all that's left is to do the easiest thing: **the right thing**.

Do the right thing, she says. You know what doing the right thing is, so now do it.

And if you don't know what the right thing is, keep reading, keep studying, until you do.

Epilogue

"Nobody exists for a reason, nobody belongs anywhere, we're all going to die" **Rick & Morty**, That's why I believe each of us should take every second of our existence and try to enjoy it and be happy. Money won't bring you happiness, but only those with money know that. There are problems everywhere in the world, but the biggest problem is limiting our perception to what only we have experienced.

People are special because of the number of moments they live and the accumulation of experiences.

We are like infinite books—books because we have a cover, an appearance, an energy that we project and that stands out, and that's what others perceive.

Our content is infinite; we can see, be, and learn whatever we want. Of course, there is a physical limit (running out of time), but I believe that reality surpasses fiction, and everything we can imagine is possible.

Discovering our place in the world is difficult when we're so conditioned by our experiences, but there's no doubt we can't lie to ourselves.

Everyone knows what they have to do; it's just a matter of doing it, without saying a word, leading by example, and in that way improving and enjoying the pleasure of achieving things through our own efforts, as a team, and with love, with a purpose that goes beyond ourselves.

There's a very fine line between being grateful and being complacent.

Only you decide when you truly enjoy who you are and what you experience, and when you're simply trapped in your comfort zone and behind a wall of anxiety that prevents you from feeling empathy and the emotions that make each day worth fighting for.

The smartest thing we can do to survive is follow the advice for growing old, but what I'm going to give you is advice for being HAPPY.

"The clever one learns from others, and the fool learns the painful way"

"The more importance we give to something, the more powerful it becomes."**LAMP**

The goal should not be to live longer, but to live a better quality of life.

No matter how old they start following them, eliminate the "what if" and let's focus on action through some of my favorite tips.

- Do what you love, even if you're bad at it.**Einstein**
- Do good without expecting anything in return; kindness is free.
- Exercise; life is better when you're handsome and attractive.
- It's easy being a parent, but it's hard being a child; call your parents more often.
- When you do altruistic acts, don't record them… you'll feel better.
- Experiment whenever you're curious, but don't do anything stupid that could put you in danger. Take the utmost care of your body and your life.
- And if you need to be in danger, or do something that goes against logic or convention to satisfy your freedom, make the people who love you understand that it's your life and you need to do what you have to do, or you'll die.

You're not alone; if you screw up, the people who love you will be screwed too. **Jose Guzman**

Loving yourself is key, but don't look down on others; humility should prevail above all else.

Those who lack morals live to discredit the morals of others, so don't follow bad paths, no matter how much they may be validated by others. **Zen P**

Study and do the right thing. **Roger Waters Mom**

Don't take things personally, don't attribute evil to mediocrity. **Carl Jung**

Luck is when opportunity and preparation converge. **Lucius Annaeus Seneca**

Do things to the best of your ability with as much passion as possible, because you never know who's watching.

All we need is love. **Canserbero**

Change your perspective and be grateful for your reality.

The last corner is love, and my advice is shaped like a triangle.

LUIS MOLERO'S TRIANGLE

Energy is what we are.

Freewill was a gift from God.

Time is our most important resource.

Happiness is what we all want.

Love is the only thing we need to obtain it.

Money is necessary to live in society.

Freedom is necessary to do what we are passionate about.

And all of this is governed by our emotional state, which can only be altered by how we perceive the cosmos.

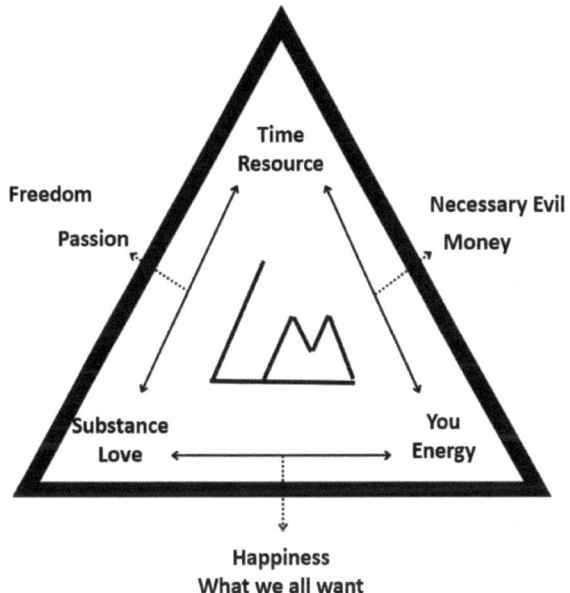

Omne Trium Perfectum Sicut Triangulum

How many triangles did you see in this book?

Index at the end

The idea behind this is simple: don't look ahead as you read the book. The intention was for you to experience it in that way, like a music album or a TV series. Seeing the song titles and episode titles diminishes some of the magic you feel when discovering events in real time. The satisfaction of using your own interpretation of things in works of art is a luxury that's greatly undervalued in such a consumerist world where everything has to be fast, explained, and delivered directly to the viewer's mind.

This is the same reason why books feel so satisfyingly different from their adaptations. Obviously, this isn't always the case, especially when there are so many good screenwriters, but for the most part, the works are better when delivered by the original author and create an almost intimate connection with the reader or viewer. Without further ado, here's the chapter layout if you need to return to a specific point.

In this new computer ecosystem where everything is a short, a reel, a tik tok, and the brain is bombarded with information, I know how hard it is to concentrate, it's an achievement that you've been able to read everything this far.

Prologue	4
TheBeginning	8
Time	16
Consciousness & Energy	19
Love	23
Freedom & Happiness	28
Money	31
언어	33
Drugs	36
Natural Laws	40
God	42
Balance	44
LAMP 12 AUG 1997	47
Life & Death	50
The Message	52
Guide for Action	54
Memento Mori	56
Future of Venezuela	58
Future of the Mundo	61
Plan of Action	63
New Enemies	65
Epilogue	68
Advice?	70
Luis Molero's triangle	72
Thank you	76
?	79

Thank you

Thank you to everyone who is a part of my life, including all the artists I listen to. To all the people who, in one way or another, have influenced me, both positively and negatively.

Thank you to my dad for his patience and boundless effort, thank you to my mom for her unconditional love and passion, thank you to my older brother for being so brave and dealing with all the problems alone, thank you to my little sister for being a role model and reminding me how much I need to improve. Thank you to my two younger siblings in Venezuela; you are the future, and I want to be better so that you have the best.

Thank you to my lifelong friends who have become my family and my brothers and sisters. I just want to be better and keep moving forward so I can have the freedom to share more moments with you.

Thanks to my country 'Venezuela' for being what it was, thanks to this country 'United States' for giving me the opportunity to rediscover myself, I promise to do what is necessary to unify this world, thanks to my grandmothers and grandfathers, I had the privilege of learning from them in their time and I will carry the legacy they left me with me forever.

Thanks to Tirone Gonzales, Marlon Morales, Pedro Elias, Roger Waters, Tomas Enrique, James Hetfield, Dan Harmon, Eiichiro Oda, Arturo Uslar, Pepe Mujica, Angel David, Jose Rafael, Led, Adrian Maximiliano, Quentin Tarantino, Hiromu Arawaka—these are some of my idols... whom we often forget are people who, just like you and me, started life crying and struggling.

Thank God for giving me what I have and for making my life a challenge I must overcome.

There aren't enough pages in the world to thank everyone I love and everything I have, so I've compressed it as much as possible.

Thanks to myself for making the decision every day to do the best I can, thanks to those who love me, and thanks to those who don't.

This was the first volume...

Now it's my turn to read, to learn from the great authors of history and nourish myself with all the relevant knowledge that has been gained over the last few thousand years.

I'm going to correct my erroneous viewpoints, which, although wrong, were necessary for who I will become.

Thank you for reading... I'd like to see your reaction, as if we could have discussed all of this.

I hope that somehow I've also managed to form a bond, a connection with you.

Maybe you're someone I know, maybe I know who you are but I don't really know you, maybe not at all, and I don't care at all.

Whoever you are, wherever you are, I want you to feel a huge hug from someone who understands that:

Philosophical polyphony

It may be better to read nothing and to run the risk of coming up with ideas that have already been proposed (like the wheel) than to be so aware of such ideas that no ideas of One's Own can develop.
Once a new idea is springs into existence it cannot be unthought there is a sense of immortality in a new idea
  Edward De Bono

The first duty of a man is to think for himself. **Jose Marti**

The diversity of men comes from culture, not from nature. On the level of instincts and psycho-physiological mechanisms, we are all basically the same. **Arturo Uslar Pietri**

The principal differences between the caveman and the modern scientists are not genetic; they are Environmental and Cultural. **Jose M. R. Delgado**

Thinking is not developed spontaneously as an expression of innate capacities; it is rather the result of a long process of learning. **H. F. Harlow**

There is no reason why we cannot teach a man to think. **B. F. Skinner**

The first duty of a government is to give education to the people. **Simon Bolivar**

The whole cannot be understood from a single point of view, which is what governments, organized religions, and authoritarian parties attempt to do. **Jiddu Krishnamurti**

A free society has always been the ultimate goal of all ideologies; there is no reason why this ideal should remain an unattainable illusion.

Rationality is not simply intelligence; it is intelligence in a free being.

Man is a being destined for freedom, who makes himself free.

The development of all people is possible. **Luis Alberto Machado**

Trauma constantly confronts us with our fragility and the inhumanity of man toward others, but also with our extraordinary resilience. Joy, creativity, meaning, and connection—all the things that make life worthwhile. Most of our energy is dedicated to connecting with others. No doctor can prescribe friendship and love. These are complex capacities that are acquired through effort. **Bessel van der Kolk**

And hope... It's not about waiting; hope is knowing that everything that is contained within you will happen and will develop. **Xavier Guix**

Development is governed by emotional state, which can only be altered by the way you perceive the cosmos, and in order to see the world from the right perspective, you have to put drops containing love into your eyes. **Alberto Molero**

The end? The beginning?
It's the same thing...It really depends on how you perceive it..
See you at volume 2

www.ingramcontent.com/pod-product-compliance
Lightning Source LLC
Chambersburg PA
CBHW042332150426
43194CB00001B/35